MODERN
SPA

C. A. M. HENNESSY
Lecturer in Modern History,
University of Exeter

HISTORICAL ASSOCIATION
London

MODERN SPAIN

The Land and the People

Spain was the first European power in modern history to acquire an Empire and the first to lose it. Spanish history since 1808 has been conditioned by the effort of readjustment to a post-Imperial epoch. Loss of Empire has meant loss of national purpose and a self-absorption in parochial issues which isolated Spain from European currents as effectively as the Inquisition had done earlier. From the seeds of the frustrated nationalism of a once great power sprang the uncertainties of the modern era and the fierce ideological conflicts which reflect only too well the obsessive introspection of Spanish intellectual life.

Spain's Empire did not strengthen the mother country economically. American silver was poured out to sustain a losing cause in Italy, on the Rhine and in the Netherlands. But for those who seek explanations for economic advance in the Protestant ethic and see the cause of Spain's decline in the frozen wealth of her religious monuments it must be remembered that Spain, in comparison with other Great Powers, is not naturally a richly endowed country. Vast areas are uninhabited and uncultivable so that, when overseas profits dried up, she was forced back on to her own poor resources.

Intractable geography has been the main determinant of Spanish history. The roots of the regional problem must be sought in physical factors. The country can be divided into areas of very high agricultural productivity such as the *huerta* of Valencia which, with its orange groves, is among the most fertile plains in Europe, and areas of poor soil and inadequate rainfall as in the *secano* of Andalusia which, together with southern Italy and parts of the Balkans, are Europe's dry-farming areas. Rainfall and soil productivity provide a key to the prevailing tenure systems and through them to political alignments.

In the Basque Provinces where rainfall is high a system of small, long-term holdings provides the infrastructure for a conservative patriarchal peasant society which has found one expression in Carlism and another in Basque nationalism. In Asturias, a land of high pastoral valleys, conditions are similar but the presence of minerals – iron in the Basque Provinces and coal in Asturias – have diversified both economies and, if Basque nationalism is the expression of one, the socialism of the Asturian miners is that of the other.

Galicia, with the country's highest rainfall, is the Ireland of Spain, a region of fishermen and peasants living on *minifundios*, the result of many generations' subdivision of the land. These *minifundios* are intensively cultivated but are barely adequate for subsistence and rarely produce a market surplus. Primitive techniques, resulting in soil depletion, have made it impossible to sustain a growing population. With the peninsula's highest birthrate Galicia is, like Ireland, a land of late marriages and cultural defensiveness and, like the Irish, the Gallegans are great migrants, both internally in domestic or casual labour and externally to the New World, especially to Argentina and Cuba where in pre-Castro days the lavish premises of the *Centro Gallego* in Havana were evidence of their worldly success. Many Gallegans, like Catalans, returned from the New World as '*americanos*' to become the region's scourge, buying up land for social prestige.

The central highlands, the *meseta* of the two Castiles, sparsely populated in scattered townships, are an area of *latifundios* and peasant holdings and the base of the wheat-growing oligarchy. The south, however, is the classic land of *latifundios*, vast estates of olive, vine and uncultivated ground. A striking feature of the latter half of the nineteenth century was the increasing predominance of Andalusians, landowners and others, in national public life as well as the emergence of rural agitation as the area's major political problem. Seasonal labour and a landless peasantry have made Andalusia the centre of the messianic agrarian anarchism which is the distinctive political feature of the Spanish south.

The well irrigated Levante supports a stable and technically advanced farm population with easy access to world markets for its citrus fruits. Valencia, the third largest city, has always been a strong republican centre, though less volatile politically than Barcelona and with fewer cultural pretensions. Catalonia, to the north, is one of the most favoured regions, with an equable climate and moderate rainfall. The humidity of Barcelona and its environs support a flourishing textile industry. In the fertile coastal plain, exporting wine, cork and agricultural products, political opinion has been radical and republican. Wide property distribution has excluded *caciquismo*,* and the peasantry has been politically involved, especially since the phylloxera of the 1880s which threatened many of the wine growers with disaster. The mountainous interior, the 'other Catalonia', has been traditionalist and was a Carlist centre in the nineteenth century; its political attitudes stemming from its inability to compete economically with the more favoured coastal regions. An important demographic fact has been the more rapid increase of Catalonia's population in relation to the rest of Spain. Inland from Catalonia, the Aragonese *meseta* provides a harsh contrast of wind-swept, rain-dry hills and here, as in Andalusia, *caciquismo* was a common phenomenon, encouraging the growth of anarchism with Zaragoza as its centre.

Much of Spain's real wealth has been and is locked away in mineral deposits – the lead mines of Cartagena, the mercury mines of Almadén which have for long held a virtual world monopoly, the iron of the Bilbao hinterland, the copper of Rio Tinto which until the challenge from the Congo and Rhodesia was a world supplier, and the wolfram, vital for armour-plated steel which, together with Moroccan iron ore, prompted much of the German interest in Spain in the 1930s. But the development of these resources has been hampered by inadequate power, lack of capital and a poor communications system. As in the case of Italy, Spanish development has been restricted by lack of coal, and although Welsh coal and Basque iron were for long complementary, lack of coal was not compensated by hydro-electric power. The harnessing of Alpine water which has turned north Italy into one of Europe's industrial complexes finds little parallel in Spain. Barcelona's industrial development has been hampered by lack of power and only recently have hydro-electric projects started to offset this traditional weakness.

Foreign capital was also slow to move into Spain – deterred by the disturbances of the 1830s and 1840s. In the 1850s and 1860s when O'Donnell's Liberal Union gave the country a measure of stability capital began to pour in, particularly from France, to finance the railway network. English money was invested in minerals – Basque and Málaga ores and Rio Tinto copper – Andalusian wines and public utilities. We know very little about Spanish

*For *caciquismo* see below, page 13. Briefly it is rule by party bosses.

investment habits – what, for example, was the effect on these of the loss of Spain's empire, what happened to the capital withdrawn from America by Spanish merchants? Some financed the sugar revolution in Cuba, but how much was re-invested in Spain itself? Perhaps much of the capital which might have gone into industrial development (Barcelona textiles from the 1830s are the exception) was diverted by the great sales of Church land, entailed estates and common lands which underpinned the Liberal revolution and helped to finance the Liberals during the Carlist wars. A *rentier* mentality inhibited the development of a dynamic liberalism, kept purchasing power low and restricted internal markets for the products of Catalan manufacturers. Unable to face competitive prices abroad the Catalans relied on internal markets and when, through the *laissez faire* policies of Madrid politicians, these were dominated by cheap Manchester cottons, Catalans became increasingly dependent on a highly protected colonial market. The movement for Iberian Union incorporating Portugal, with its anglophobic undercurrent, which erupted in mid-century and again in the 1870s, had as one of its purposes the enlarging of the domestic market.

Communications were amongst the worst in Europe. Fast-flowing or dried-up rivers reduced river transport to a minimum. Roads, in spite of the imaginative road-building programme of Charles III's ministers, deteriorated through want of upkeep. Mules, even today, remain a staple means of transport for the rural population. Although by the 1870s the main towns had been linked by the railway system it soon became inadequate. Single-track lines created bottlenecks such as the Depeñaperros pass, the main link with Andalusia, whilst the uneconomic radiation of the system from Madrid did not increase efficiency. Freight charges remained high and became a major political issue at the end of the century. In fact, 'railway politics', as in the various scandals over concessions in the 1840s and 1870s, could always be counted on to add spice to parliamentary life.

The Revolution of 1868

In September 1868 the long reign of the Bourbon Isabella II was brought to an end by a revolt of discontented generals and civilian politicians. The wilfulness of the queen in choosing ministers and granting dissolutions as well as the increasing power of her clerical advisers goaded the persecuted Liberal opposition into revolt, and economic depression assured the conspirators of mass support. After a comparatively bloodless revolution, spreading out from Cádiz, the classic home of Spanish liberalism, Isabella went into exile. Although the September Revolution was not to be the Spanish 1789, as many contemporaries hoped, it released pent up energies which were to make the next six years a period of tumultuous political experiment. Finally tiring of political anarchy, which had led to a three-sided civil war, the country welcomed Alfonso XII as the new king in 1874 almost as enthusiastically as it had expelled his mother six years before.

The 1868 Revolution was the masterstroke of one man – General Prim, the hero of the Moroccan war of 1859, whose thwarted political ambitions turned him into Isabella's most dangerous enemy. Without Prim's persistence there would have been no revolution. He proved himself a competent statesman but circumstances defied him. It was not until 1870, after a humiliating search, that he succeeded in persuading a foreign prince, Amadeo of Savoy, to accept the throne. But at the moment when Amadeo arrived in Spain Prim was assassinated – a historical mystery which still awaits solution. Some believe that his death put the seal on Amadeo's reign and that but for this Amadeo would not have been forced to abdicate two years later. But this is scarcely realistic. Prim was a prisoner of his own revolution. It was naïve to expect the instrument of that revolution, the army officers, to stand down and don frock coats as Prim himself did. The army was the kingmaker of Spanish politics and men like Prim or General Pavía, whose Brumaire-style coup brought the First Republic to an end in 1874, but who refused to 'become a Cromwell', were exceptions to the rule. What made Prim's task doubly difficult was the fortuitous outbreak, only ten days after Isabella's overthrow, of the Cuban War of Independence which was to drag on for a decade. Unable to reduce the army's power, Prim was soon faced by a virulent republican exploitation of anti-militarism which made him further dependent on army protection.

The army's role in Spanish politics has sociological roots. Unlike contemporary Prussia or England the aristocracy had long contracted out of military service. During and after the War of Independence the army became an open field for the ambitious ranker – Espartero and Prim, to take the two greatest *caudillos* of the nineteenth century, were the sons of a peasant and a chemist respectively. The army provided for social mobility – a bastardized form of the career open to talents but one where the talents were not those of military efficiency but of political calculation. The army was also a bureaucratic institution in a country plagued by *empleomania*, the rage for office, providing careers for a middle class with few openings in industry or commerce. As a result the officer-men ratio was ludicrously high with pay correspondingly low. The penurious officers of the Spanish novel have their counterparts in real life. Promotion blockages and the expense of keeping a family made many susceptible to the approaches of conspiring politicians.

In 1868 the deteriorating situation in Cuba gave the army a continuing interest in politics. The Reform movement which might have solved the Cuban problem by granting a measure of autonomy to the island had failed by 1868 when a new tax law and administrative reforms goaded into revolt the economically backward landowners of Oriente province who were least able to bear the new burdens. Like the *colons* in Algeria in the 1950s the '*peninsulares*' of Cuba – poor white immigrants, bureaucrats and Spanish merchants – were strong enough to negate any liberalizing tendencies of the home government or any attempt to find a compromise solution. Prim's diplomatic manoeuvring with the United States also exposed him to the attacks of his opponents at home. The 'defence of the integrity of the territory' became the rallying cry for frustrated nationalists, the unscrupulous politicians looking for a platform and the highly protected flour and textile exporters who feared that any weakening of Spanish control would throw Cuba into the economic orbit of the United States, as indeed it was to do. In terms of domestic politics the war meant that the army had to be expanded. The unfair conscription system which bore heavily on those who could not afford redemption payments enabled the republicans to build up a mass following and to become the most dangerous source of opposition to the revolutionary settlement.

A further justification for the army's political role was found when the Carlist revival led to open warfare in 1872. From the 1830s onwards Carlism had become the refuge of anti-liberal traditionalists. Between 1833 and 1839 Carlist levies had fought Liberal armies to a standstill in the mountains of northern Spain. Closely linked to the defence of the local privileges (*fueros*) of the

Basque Provinces and Navarre, Carlism was the political expression of an inward and backward looking patriarchal society which resented any disturbance of its traditional way of life. Its revival was stimulated by the granting of freedom of worship in the constitution of 1869, which threatened Catholic unity. At the same time the fall of the senior Bourbon line encouraged the collateral line to make a bid for power. When the parliamentary wing of the party was overruled in 1872, the Carlist bands took to arms, tying down the army in a four year civil war. Carlism was the only mass movement in nineteenth-century Spain worthy of the name. But after the peace of 1876 much of its energy was drawn into regionalist movements and the unity of the old Carlist areas was broken by the development of industry in the Basque Provinces which left rural Navarre as the last stronghold of Carlist traditionalism and later the source of some of Franco's most reliable troops.

The Republicans alone of political parties attacked the army but in this they were too successful. Their corrosive anti-militarism sapped the army's discipline at the moment when they most needed it in order to defend the new régime from left-wing extremists in the south and Carlist attacks in the north. Republicanism, an urban movement, anti-militarist, anti-clerical, and led by intellectuals, was the first political movement in Spain to try to mobilize mass opinion. Its strength lay in its federal principles which appealed particularly to the Mediterranean coast towns which resented the domination of Madrid. But federalism remained a localized phenomenon and, however idealistic its leaders may have been, the majority of its followers, under-employed lawyers and provincial petty bourgeoisie, were attracted mainly by the opportunities for jobbery which a decentralized federal system seemed to offer. A major weakness, too, was the division between a socialist and anti-socialist wing which was made more acute by the appearance of Bakuninist anarchism after 1868. The aftermath of the Paris Commune gave many republicans second thoughts, particularly as Spain seemed on the point of becoming the centre of the International's activities in Europe. When the Republicans finally came to power in 1873, after four years' opposition in parliament and on the barricades, it was not through a popular revolutionary uprising but because of the collapse of the monarchists whose king, despairing of ruling constitutionally, threw in his hand. Republican failures then forced the army's hand. Early in 1874 an army coup overthrew the government and, although the Republic lingered on, its weakness and lack of support prompted another army coup at the end of the year in favour of the restored Bourbon monarchy under Isabella's son, Alfonso.

THE RESTORATION: 1874–1923

Although army generals had engineered the coup, the architect of the Restoration was a civilian politician, Cánovas del Castillo. Until his assassination in 1897 Cánovas dominated Spanish politics. Like the Republican leaders he was an intellectual but his inspiration was not, like theirs, Proudhon and the German metaphysicians but the realities of Spanish history. A two-volume study of the age of Spanish decadence in the seventeenth century and participation in politics ever since he had been O'Donnell's civilian adviser in the Revolution of 1854 had made him pessimistic about the capacity of Spaniards for self-government. He was a doctrinaire liberal, believing in a strong monarchy and a restricted franchise. His liberalism was sincere even if his application of it seemed cynical. He believed Spain needed to be educated to the idea of parliamentary government and to the concept of a monarch above parties. Bemused by English parliamentarianism, he wanted to create a two-party system but because of the fissiparous tendencies of Spanish politics he came to believe that this could only be achieved by an agreement between the two main parties to rotate in office. In this way the spoils of office could be shared and a responsible opposition built up. In many ways this was a more realistic solution to the problems of factionalism than the *trasformismo* of his Italian contemporary, Depretis. To both men politics was not an activity for resolving ideological questions but a machinery for satisfying legitimate desires for power and the financial fruits deriving from them. Cánovas's '*turnismo*' was, moreover, designed to eradicate the evil of *retraimiento*, the device by which opposition parties withdrew from the Cortes so as to remove the only catalyst which could unite the governing party. However, like the Confederations of eighteenth-century Poland, this withdrawal was usually a prelude to armed revolt.

The basic presupposition of *turnismo* was that elections would be arranged beforehand and for this there had to be shared common ground between the two party leaders. Cánovas was fortunate in finding in Sagasta a man who would play this role. Unlike Cánovas, Sagasta had been an active participant in the 1868 Revolution, but he had been outmanoeuvred by his more radical colleagues. He represented the views of those behind the 1869 Constitution and Cánovas's understanding with him, which was clinched in the Pact of El Pardo on Alfonso's death in 1885, reflected his desire to leave no element excluded from political life.

In addition to a reconciliation with the men of 1869 Cánovas aimed also to reconcile the Church with liberalism. Like Giolitti in Italy later, he was harassed by an intransigent Catholic sector whose Bible was the 1864 Syllabus of Errors. The Carlists were more Catholic than the pope, but by giving his support to the restored Bourbons the latter reduced them to a dynastic rump whose internal divisions and the incompetence of their leader left them powerless. The triumph of Cánovas's reconciliation policy was his incorporation of the ex-Carlist Pidal into parliamentary life at the head of his *Unión Nacional* party.

The Constitution of 1876, the Restoration charter, guaranteed religious freedom. It tolerated the *Libre Institución de Enseñanza* which graduated a whole generation of anti-clerical intellectuals; but by lax interpretation of the 1851 Concordat it also allowed new religious orders into Spain. In fact, Spain gave shelter to many of the Catholic orders which were driven out of France by Ferry's anti-clericalism. Thus it was during Cánovas's period of domination that a new polarization between clericals and anti-clericals began to form. The paradox of Cánovas's liberalism was that he indirectly encouraged the development of the forces of clericalism and anti-clericalism, neither of which were prepared to accept the doctrinaire attitude of the *juste milieu*.

The linch-pin of the Restoration system was the monarch whose vital function was the power of dissolution. As public opinion as expressed in the Cortes was a fiction, the task of deciding when a government had lost the nation's confidence was not an easy one. The surprising thing was that it worked so well, not only under Alphonso XII who was Cánovas's protégé but also under the Regent, Maria Christina. One of the causes of the collapse of the *turnismo* system was the wilfulness of the young Alfonso XIII (whose coming-of-age in 1902 coincided with the disappearance from political life of the old party leaders) in granting dissolutions. Without the monarch's co-operation Cánovas's system was a mockery.

The army too had to co-operate, and perhaps Cánovas's greatest achievement was his feat of keeping the army out of politics. In spite of his efforts, the Restoration had been engineered by generals but they failed both to consolidate this advantage or to exploit the victory over the Carlists and remained on the fringes of political life until after Cánovas's death. Here again the monarch played a key role. Cánovas deliberately built the king into a military figure, with the Kaiser as his model, and in this way attached the loyalty of the army to the king's person. Martínez Campos, who had staged the coup which restored the Bourbons, was posted to Cuba but even after his success in bringing the Ten Years' War to an end by the compromise Peace of Zanjón in 1878, he was unable to exercise decisive political influence. As in the hey-day of O'Donnell's imperialism in the 1860s, army involvement in campaigns and garrison duty abroad helped to remove the threat of political involvement at home.

But although Cuba served a useful political function by absorbing potential undesirables, it was the Cuban question which finally provoked the greatest crisis of Cánovas's career. The peace of 1878 was only a breathing space. The war had effectively destroyed the old slave plantation system and when slavery was abolished in 1880 the main factor inhibiting the nationalist leaders was removed. A new generation of leaders among the Cuban nationalists rejected the compromise solutions which had come too late and in 1895 full-scale war broke out again. This time it proved impossible for the Spaniards to contain the revolt in the eastern end of the island except through a war of attrition which turned Cuba into a howling wilderness. What threatened to become a stalemate was broken by the intervention of the United States in 1898 and in a sharp war of seven months the last of Spain's colonies outside Africa were lost. The 'Disaster of '98' was a traumatic experience for the country which had been lulled into a false sense of security by the very stability of the restoration régime.

The colonial disaster brought to the surface the submerged forces which had been germinating ever since the economic boom collapsed in the late 1880s – regionalism, anti-clericalism, militant anarchism, army frustration and a general *fin de siècle* pessimism which reacted violently against the clichés of parliamentary liberalism. Sorel's doctrine of violence, Anarchist utopianism and a hankering after a Nietzschean superman were the intellectual fodder of the younger generation – ingredients scarcely conducive to the survival of a parliamentary system. Regenerationist literature pumped new breath into the time-worn theme of traditionalism versus Europeanization, and although corrupt politics was generally felt to have been responsible for Spain's decline, there was also a call for the eradication of root causes. Particularly vocal in this respect was Joaquin Costa for whom the solution lay in education and hydraulics. His attempt to break the political stalemate by founding a new party – the *Unión Nacional* – by appealing to the provincial and rural bourgeoisie never got off the ground.

The political bankruptcy of the Restoration settlement was due to the failure of *turnismo* to evolve into a genuine two-party system as Cánovas had hoped. When the two key figures died – Cánovas in 1897 and Sagasta in 1903 – and the ablest of their contemporaries, Silvela, retired from active politics in 1904, the common ground of shared experience was lost. Memories of the 1868–74 fiascos had conditioned the Cánovas – Sagasta compromise, but by the opening decade of the twentieth century new forces had erupted which needed to be incorporated into the nation's political life. This might have been achieved in 1890 when Sagasta's government brought back manhood suffrage, but instead of this giving the new forces a reflection in parliament it merely served to fortify the system of *caciquismo*. Although by the second decade of the new century republicans and socialists were beginning to be returned to the Cortes for the larger towns, the party bosses still ruled the rural areas.

The key political figures of the Restoration period were the civil governors, *jefes políticos* (political bosses) in the towns, and the *caciques*, the rural party bosses, who were responsible for ensuring that the right candidates were returned at elections. *Caciquismo* is a fundamental part of modern Spanish political life. By patronage, pressure and physical violence the *caciques* were the guarantee that free elections would remain a fiction. Only where, as in Catalonia, security of tenure had produced an independent peasantry was *caciquismo* unimportant. Politics were personalist, dependent on an intricate network of patronage relationships in which the *enchufe* (literally a plug-in) or the right contact, was all-important. Corruption in a society still dominated by the extended family concept did not carry the same stigma as in our own society. Loyalty to the in-group and to the *patria chica* more often than no came before loyalty to the impersonal state.

Yet although discredited, the parliamentary régime survived until the military coup of 1923. A dominating political figure of this period, the heir to Cánovas and Sagasta, was Antonio Maura, who tried to breathe life into the 1876 Constitution and to bridge the gap between the legal and real life of the country. A natural conservative who had been much influenced by 'regenerationism', Maura planned for a 'revolution from above'. Spain's crisis, he believed, was one of governing élites. But his position was paradoxical. Like Costa, he needed the co-operation of the 'neutral masses', the provincial bourgeoisie and peasantry, which except in Catalonia held aloof from politics. His curious choice of La Cierva, a reactionary and an agile election fixer, as Minister of the Interior, ran counter to his own attempts to root out *caciquismo,* and Maura's Local Government Bill, designed to destroy the caciques' power, never became law. He was a solitary figure, a clerical in a period of rising anti-clericalism, a centralist when Catalan regionalism was turning into a strident nationalism, and a believer in a directed revolution within the framework of a system which would have been among the first casualties of his reforms. Maura's revolution posited a quiescent or accommodating working class and a middle class prepared to put national interests before those of the region. When Maura finally threw in his hand at the end of his ministry in 1922, saying 'Let those who prevent government govern', he confessed the inability of parliamentary liberalism to survive within the terms of the Restoration settlement and in face of those sectionalist forces which could not be incorporated within it.

If the invertebrate nature of Spanish society was a reason for the weakness of Spanish parliamentary liberalism, it was also a reason for the weakness and disorganization of the vital forces which might have provided a viable opposition. Most striking were the divisions on the Left among the mass parties of the urban and rural working class. Working class organizations date effectively from 1868. The anarchists were first in the field, more by accident than by design, when the Italian follower of Bakunin, Fanelli, appearing in Barcelona in October 1868, swept his audience off their feet by moral exhortations in a language none of his hearers could understand. Once established in Barcelona, anarchism kept its hold, despite the efforts of Marx's Cuban son-in-law, Lafargue, to displace it by Marxism.

The authoritarian atmosphere of Madrid made it more susceptible to Marxist overtures and the founding there in 1879 of a Marxist-orientated Socialist party perpetuated the initial division, at the same time introducing into working class politics the regional pattern which characterized middle class political activity. Why anarcho-syndicalism rather than socialism should have become so firmly rooted in highly industrialized Catalonia has not been satisfactorily explained. It may have been partly due to the influence of migrant Andalusian workers bringing with them the messianic expectations of agrarian anarchism, partly to the repressive atmosphere of Catalan industry run by harsh self-made businessmen. Scorning the compromises of parliamentary politics, the anarchists also rejected the economic expediency of wage bargaining. For them the strike was a political weapon to be used without regard to success or failure in a continuous process of tempering the revolutionary spirit of the masses. The great Saragossa strike of 1934 lasted for fifty-seven days and that without strike pay. Unlike the Socialists whose rationale attracted many prominent middle-class intellectuals, the anarchists were a closed society with their own mystique and a sect mentality with apocalyptic expectations. Yet for all their moral fervour they should not be over-idealized. The ruthlessness of some of their leaders has few parallels in modern history; men like Durruti and Ascaso were specialists in political assassination, and it is often difficult to draw the line between political terrorism and mere gangsterism.

Socialism took longer to establish itself. Lacking the industrial base of Barcelona, Madrid socialism was an affair of artisans, skilled workers, particularly typographers, middle-class intellectuals and later white collar workers, especially bank clerks. In 1888 the socialist union, the UGT (*Unión General de Trabajadores*), was formed. Although slow in expanding it claimed a membership of a quarter of a million by 1918. Outside Madrid the strongest area of support was in Bilbao and its hinterland and in the coal-mining areas of Asturias. But even authoritarian Spanish socialism was rent by internal divisions – particularly between Largo Caballero, the self-educated plasterer who succeeded Iglesias, the party's founder, in 1925 and Indalecio Prieto. Caballero felt acutely the need for intransigence if the Socialists were to hold their own against the Anarchists, but Prieto, whose early journalism had brought him contacts among the Bilbao plutocracy, was more flexible and accommodating.

The most complex as well as the most explosive issue was the growth of regionalist feeling. 'Liberal Spain' was a phenomenon of the heartland, where an artificial capital was dominated by Castilian and Andalusian landowners and their political clients. Madrid's supremacy had formerly been that of an Imperial Court, but this was unrealistic now that the nation's wealth was no longer drawn from the silver mines of Potosí and Guanajuato but from the industrial complexes of Bilbao and Barcelona. Regionalism was a peripheral movement, a revolt against the Liberals' attempts to centralize administration and to rule in the interests of the metropolis. In Galicia, where it was least important, it was a 'Celtic fringe' phenomenon of provincial intellectuals, an amalgam of nostalgia and romance where the determined leadership which might have canalized the resentment of the Galician peasants was lacking. There were few comparable Galician equivalents to the Catalan peasants whose radicalism stemmed from the depression caused by the phylloxera outbreak in the 1880s. In the Basque Provinces, regionalism had more pronounced cultural, linguistic and racial roots. If at first it drew its sustenance from the ex-Carlists' longing for a lost paradise, it was soon taken up by the Bilbao plutocracy. Still monarchist until the republican championship of regional autonomy, Basque regionalism reflected the growing prosperity of an area which had developed its own heavy industrial complex and a financial power which gave Bilbao banks a foothold in every sizeable Spanish town.

Whereas Basque regionalism with its progressive Catholicism and comparative absence of class strife is a fairly straightforward phenomenon, Catalan regionalism is the most complex of modern Spanish problems. Nourished by a linguistic revival and a literary renaissance which gave Barcelona a justifiable claim to be the cultural capital of Spain, it was both more open to European influences and more sensitive to the colonial crisis. Bolstering their arguments with historical grievances, real and imagined, Catalan nationalists could see no redress short of autonomy. The driving force came from the Catalan bourgeoisie which, since the opening of the Spanish-American ports in the 1770s, had regained its fifteenth-century reputation as the most dynamic social group in the peninsula. The 'Manchester of Spain' had experienced an industrial revolution based on textiles which bred an optimism resentful of checks from Madrid. But the issue was not clear cut. Not only were there different trends within Catalan regionalism, such as the Catholic traditionalism of towns like

Vich and the radical anti-clericalism of Ampurdan with its booming cork-economy; there were also acute social tensions which, made Barcelona the European revolutionary city *par excellence*. These social tensions acted as a brake on the nationalist leaders. The complications of Catalan politics stem, in large measure, from the middle-class fear of the militant anarchist-infected working class which could be manipulated by Madrid to tame recalcitrant nationalists.

Complaints that Madrid's *laissez faire* policies were ruining Catalan industry began in the early 1840s but reached a climax after the 1868 revolution which inaugurated a free-trade régime. This was the signal for a massive Catalan drive for protection and it was partly the exploitation of this grievance which enabled the Federals to make Barcelona the strongest Republican centre in Spain, although the experience of the First Republic cured much of the Barcelona middle class of its political illusions. Cuba played a vital part in the Catalan economy. Soap, cork, sacks, wines, shipping and textiles were among the many interests involved, in addition to the large Catalan colony in the island which had almost pre-empted Cuban economic life, and through which capital flowed back into Catalonia. War, whether the Franco-Prussian War, the Cuban War of Independence or the War of 1914–18, meant a boom for Catalan industry, but the loss of Cuba brought to an end an artificially protected market and internal markets were insufficient to absorb the flow of goods. Cut-backs in industrial production created the mass discontent in Barcelona which provided the rising demagogue and brash young politician Lerroux with the raw material for his new style radicalism in the same way as the cut-backs after the Great War gave a sharper edge to the city's social conflicts.

The failure to absorb Catalan regionalism into the existing political system opened the dyke to new disruptive forces. Lerroux's game of working with Madrid politicians against the nationalist parties was a dangerous one. The volatile radicalism of the 'Emperor of the Parallelo', the red-light quarter of Barcelona, could be turned to other purposes. The son of an army vet., and middle class to the core, Lerroux was the prototype of the inspired Latin demagogue. But his importance should not be underestimated. Republicanism after 1873 was a spent force, an affair of frock-coated intellectuals and a handful of conspirators who, turning their backs on republican tradition, attempted to 'work' discontented army officers. Lerroux cut republicanism away from the measured cadences of Castelar, from Salmerón's sectarianism, from Pi y Margall's austere rigidity; he sensed new possibilities for a dynamic republicanism with violent anticlericalism as its main ingredient and wild appeals to the destructive instinct. Lerroux's day came during the 'Tragic Week' of 1909, the first of the great Barcelona crises which were to rock Spanish politics during the next fifteen years.

The Tragic Week of violent rioting, caused by the attempt to call up reservists for a Moroccan campaign, exposed the thin veneer of Barcelona's respectability and highlighted the dilemma of the nationalist parties. Ultimately their security depended on army power but the army was centralist and anti-Catalan. After 1909 the alliance of the Catalan parties which had been formed in 1906 broke up and Cambó's Lliga, the party of the industrialists, felt its way to an understanding with the army which was preparing its political comeback. Two choices lay open to the army – either to associate with the Renovation movement of nationalist and Left parties whose criticisms of corrupt politicians the military shared, or to act by itself. The officers chose the latter course when they set up the *Juntas de Defensa* to protect army interests in a period of rising prices and anti-militarism. This was sectionalism run riot; the officers had become the prisoners of their trade union mentality. The army's ruthless suppression of the general strike of 1917 showed up both its isolation from public opinion and the extent to which governments were dependent on its power. The bitter sordid years in Barcelona after 1917 consolidated its hold. With martial law the army became the maker and breaker of cabinets. It only needed a deteriorating situation in Morocco to force the army's hand and for Primo de Rivera to make his coup of 1923.

From Primo de Rivera to Franco: Alfonso XIII and the Second Republic

Primo de Rivera has sometimes been described (by Alfonso XIII among others) as the 'Mussolini of Spain'. Nothing could be further from the truth. There was no march on Rome, no blackshirted militia, no organized terrorism, and none of the ideological pretentiousness of the Italian dictator. As Captain-General of Catalonia in 1923 where the army's rule was law, Primo was a natural figure to make a coup and so shield the king from the damaging revelations of the inquiry into the causes of the disaster of Anual in 1921 when a Spanish army of 7,000 soldiers had been massacred by the Moors. A week before the commission was to have reported Primo made his coup. Force was not required: the parliamentary régime had ground to a halt, discredited by its Moroccan and Catalan failures. For the first two years, 1923–5, Primo ruled with a military junta, employing soldiers in state-subsidized concerns much as Perón was to do later.

In Catalonia itself, Conservatives saw a military dictatorship as an insurance against the social revolution which had been threatening since 1917. Nor was Primo generally unpopular; he was eminently *simpático* – an Andalusian *señorito*, with none of the haughty pride of that class. He was voluble, genial, with the natural vices to endear him with that large part of the population which admired *hombría*. Working in fitful starts, he was the arch-pragmatist of Spanish politics, believing in simplistic solutions: government was a matter of eloquence and common sense, with the hard work of economic decisions left to his youthful and brilliant finance minister, Calvo Sotelo.

The fundamental flaw in his régime, quite apart from its unconstitutionality, was its institutional weakness. His failure to win over the old politicians postponed the early return to normality he had anticipated when he came to power. By 1926, when he was growing restive at his own unconstitutionalism, he tried to create a new party, the *Unión Patriótica* and, influenced by Fascist corporatism, he set up a corporative assembly in 1927 to prepare a constitution to be submitted to a plebiscite in 1931. This, however, was never to take place.

Primo's rule until a year before his fall in 1930 was smoothed by the economic boom which made the mid-1920s an Indian summer for speculators. It was to become a byword for public works and a halcyon period for some foreign investors. At the same time Primo entered into a close understanding with the Socialists, who probably accepted this strange alliance in the hope of gaining ground from the Anarchists who had been proscribed. With such favourable conditions his régime was an era of unrivalled industrial peace.

Peace in Morocco, a tamed labour movement and economic progress were secured at the expense of political freedom. When the revolt against the dictatorship came, it was primarily a revolt of the middle class with the intellectuals and the army particularly restive. True to his type, Primo had no time for intellectuals. Uninterested in the problems of education, he was happy to allow Church influence in the schools to increase. Universities which protested at interference with their regulations were closed, thus turning professors and students into his most active opponents. As in the 1860s, Spanish intellectuals in exile became the spear-head of the opposition, whilst students inside Spain, taking a cue from the Latin-American university reform movement, began to emerge as a self-conscious political group. The army, particularly the artillery officers who resented an infantryman's attempts to interfere with their privileges, was no longer prepared to bear the odium of a régime which could not be liberalized. When Primo, tired and disillusioned with the failure of his new-style party, was dismissed and withdrew to a self-imposed exile in 1930, General Berenguer tried to undertake the most difficult of all political exercises, the liberalization of a dictatorship. But Primo's historical function had been to protect the king against his critics and once he had gone Alfonso was exposed to the full blast of republican criticism led by the great names of Spanish intellectual life.

The Republic was voted in on the urban vote at the municipal elections of April 1931. Alfonso abdicated without even waiting for the final results to come in from the rural areas, although these would have shown an overall monarchist majority. This time the birth of the Republic was not a shabby backstairs political intrigue, as in February 1873, but a mammoth demonstration of optimistic hope in the potentialities of a republican régime. Although military republicanism stood in the wings, it was not called on: the significant fact in April 1931 was that this was the first régime to be ushered in without the active intervention of the army.

The strongest group in the Constituent Cortes, as might be expected, was the republican parties among which must be included the Socialists. With 120 out of 450 deputies they were the largest single party, and for once their leaders were agreed on a reformist platform of participation in the government. The 'pure' republican parties, grouped round Azaña's comparatively small Republican Action, consisted of the Radical Socialists, the Federalists – an echo of 1873 – and Lerroux's Radicals on the right wing of the Republican bloc. These parties broadly represented the middle and lower middle groups in favour of a moderate republic with enough social reform to stave off social revolution but not enough to disturb the tenets of a property-owning democracy. In addition, the republicans had allies in the nationalist parties, the Catalan Esquerra and the Gallegan Home Rulers. The Basque nationalists, through Catholic conviction, voted with the smaller Rightist groups. The small representation of the traditional Spanish ruling groups in the Constituent Cortes gave a false impression of the strength of republicanism and also enabled Lerroux to trim his sails to the wind of rising Catholic opinion outside the Cortes.

Until the outbreak of civil war five years later politics divided into three main periods: until mid-1933, the Constituent Cortes dominated by progressive republicanism; from November 1933 to February 1936, the *Bienio Negro*, the 'black two years' of right wing republicanism; from February until July 1936, the period of the Popular Front during which the polarization of political forces led to civil war.

The two years of the Constituent Cortes was the gilded period of the republic. Over half the deputies came from the professional groups (123 lawyers, 65 professors, and 41 doctors) which formed the backbone of republican support. This was the republic of the intellectuals, idealistic, politically immature, shortsighted and with mistaken priorities. The absence of a governing tradition, an inefficient bureaucracy and the lack of consensus for a moderate republic soon punctured exaggerated hopes and led to the early disillusion of many of the country's finest brains. Azaña, the prime minister, typified this early period. An intellectual recluse, lonely and morose, his virtue was an incorruptibility which even his enemies grudgingly admitted, his vice a weakness for epigrams more suitable for the Ateneo debating club than for the leading minister. The President, Alcalá Zamora, a Catholic and conservative republican, might have been a guarantee of the government's moderation, but his powers had been drastically curtailed through fear of the executive abusing the right of dissolution as the monarchy had done. Moreover, the absence of a Second Chamber removed another check on the Legislature. In retrospect, the main criticism of the Constituent Cortes was not so much that it was too radical but that it was radical in the wrong places, alienating potential supporters without winning over those who might have been its most ardent defenders.

The touchstone of the republicans' intentions rested on their treatment of the four main outstanding problems – the Church, the army, regionalism and the land. Republican reactions to the first three were pre-packaged: anti-clericalism, anti-militarism and decentralization were part of the ill-defined tradition of Spanish republicanism. The land problem, however, required more than a Pavlovian reflex and it was here that the republicans lacked decisiveness and showed the limitations of their outlook.

If Primo had been fortunate in coming to power in a period of economic expansion, the Republic suffered by being the heir to the Depression. The peseta was not stabilized until 1934; agricultural prices fell and unemployment rose as land went out of cultivation. Contracting markets for primary products underlined the urgent need for a quick solution to the agrarian crisis, the most serious problem faced by the new Republic. But regional variations and the lack of technicians precluded a swift solution, and even so progress was slower than might have been expected. The Agrarian Law which at first applied only to the central and southern provinces was passed comparatively easily in 1932. By this, unworked estates over 56 acres were to be expropriated by the Institute of Agrarian Reform which would administer compensation payments and arrange for land distribution either to individuals or to co-operatives. But by 1934 only 12,500 had been settled, and during the Lerroux administration of the same year funds were withdrawn from the Institute of Agrarian Reform.

Part of the trouble lay in the fact that, like their predecessors of the 1870s, republicans were urban-minded, uninterested in and largely misinformed about conditions in the *campo*. Much more could have been learnt from the experience of the Mexican Revolution where similar problems were being faced at the same time, but in fact the Republicans did little to heal the traditional breach between town and country. For radical republicans anti-clericalism was the major issue, so whilst energies went into doctrinaire anti-clericalism which alienated many potential supporters initiative in the countryside passed into the hands of extremists. Reformers were in any case divided over agrarian policy. Republicans thought in terms of distributing plots to individual owners which would give the republic a political base in an independent peasantry after the style of the Third Republic in France, whereas the Socialists argued for a collectivist solution. The socialist approach was more in keeping with the realities of the dry-farming area of the central meseta and Andalusia where the agrarian problem was most acute and where only the pooling of resources could provide a viable solution; but a rational solution is not necessarily the viable one where the driving force of discontent is land-hunger.

Republican anti-clericalism, resulting in the separation of church and state and a permissive attitude to morality, was a reaction to the close dependence of the church on the state during the monarchy. Doctrinaire anti-clericalism was a rehash of nineteenth-century views, much as the Church's thinking was a hangover of an earlier period, especially on social questions. However understandable, the republican attitude played into the hands of the Right as well as creating a crisis of conscience for many of its Catholic supporters.

The anti-Catalan policies of Primo had strengthened Catalan republicanism which was now exemplified most forcefully by Colonel Maciá and his Esquerra, the left-wing nationalist organization which had drawn support away from Cambó's Lliga. For a moment it even looked as if Catalonia might become an independent state, and as in 1873 it required a deputation from the Cortes to restrain separatist enthusiasm. Although the government parties were determined to grant autonomy to Catalonia it was only after a bitter rearguard action by the Right that the Catalan Statute was finally passed in September 1932.

Those most aggrieved by Azaña's Catalan policy were the army officers who felt that the army's achievement in Catalonia between 1917 and 1923 had been undone; but, sensitive though Catalonia might be as a touchstone of army opinion, there were other more tangible factors to alienate officers from the new régime. The Republicans' anti-militarism was notorious. Azaña's abolition of the cherished Law of Jurisdictions of 1905 exposed the army to a taunting anti-military press. The power of Captains-General was severely restricted; breaches of the civil code by soldiers now came under the jurisdiction of ordinary courts; and although the number of officers compulsorily retired removed promotion blockages, thus winning over junior officers, officers retired on full pay with time on their hands made combustible revolutionary material. This found expression in the Union Militar Española (UME), a cabal of officers linked to various right-wing factions; and in 1932 General Sanjurjo, outraged at the Catalan Statute, staged the first *pronunciamiento* against the Republic at Seville. It had only needed sixteen months of the Republic to cool Sanjurjo's republican ardour.

Of the pressing problems facing the Republic during the Constituent period only the Catalan problem had been satisfactorily solved. Little had been done to reassure the military or to provide an effective counterweight to the army, and a hasty anti-clerical policy had rallied the disparate forces of the Right. Finally, the failure of the government to implement agrarian reform and its mishandling of the Casas Viejas affair (when an anarchist group in Andalusia was liquidated by the Civil Guard) broke the alliance between the republicans and the socialists on which the political equilibrium had rested for the past two years. By the end of 1933 the early optimism was already dimmed, and political momentum passed to a new party, the CEDA, whose republican sympathies seemed, to the Left at least, open to question, and to an old party, the Radicals, whose opportunism had swung it from enthusiastic to grudging republicanism and whose leader, Lerroux, was an old-style politician from the discredited monarchist past.

The 1933 elections revealed that universal suffrage, as had happened in the Second French Republic, does not necessarily produce a radical majority. The breakdown of the republican-socialist understanding was one reason for the swing to the Right, but the introduction of votes for women also proved political suicide for the republican parties once anti-clericalism had become an electoral issue. This was capitalized by a new party, highly organized and well-endowed, the CEDA (*Confederación Española de Derechos Autónomas*), an alliance of right-wing groups and the brain-child of the Jesuits. CEDA and its leader, Gil Robles, owed some of its inspiration to the German Centre party, some to Dollfuss in Austria. Gil Robles's republican sincerity has been questioned, and although the new party claimed to be a Catholic party of the masses in a conservative republic the monarchism and reactionary nature of affiliated groups like *Renovación Española* and the Traditionalists was so notorious as to give these doubts some substance. The Radicals, whose name belied their convictions, also increased their following until they were the largest party. Lerroux, now comfortably conservative, became the arbiter of politics and formed the government during the Bienio Negro.

CEDA was too closely dependent on the funds of large landowners to be anything more than a front for the Right. However, as CEDA did not have an overall majority in the Cortes the Radicals formed a centre government. Immediately much of the legislation of the Constituent Cortes was reversed, agrarian reform was soft-pedalled, educational reform was slowed down, rebel officers amnestied. Lerroux was, in fact, in no position to pursue an independent policy, but his apparent capitulation to the Right produced an immediate response from the Anarchists who staged a rising at Saragossa in December, followed by the great strike of March 1934. This new wave of anarchist militancy spurred the Socialists to action. Their recent increase of strength among the agrarian masses was threatened by the breakdown of the reform programme, and unless they made an attempt to outbid the Anarchists they would be in danger of losing all their gains. Thus the Socialist party, under Largo Caballero's lead, moved from reform to revolution. The admission of three CEDA members to the government provided the pretext for a general strike which turned into armed revolt. Quickly snuffed in Madrid and Barcelona, the brunt was borne by the Socialist Asturian coal-miners of Oviedo. But the significance of the October rising in Asturias was that, for the first time, the various working-class organizations were united. The epic resistance, the harsh suppression, the exaggerated atrocity stories, make October 1934 a turning point in the Republic's history.

The weakness and financial scandals of the Lerroux administration provided CEDA with the long-awaited chance to form a government, but they were baulked by the President who, rather than turn to Gil Robles, dissolved the Cortes, fixing elections for February 1936. As the electoral law in 1933 had favoured the Right, so in 1936 it favoured the parties of the Left which, following the example of the *Alianza Obrera* of 1934, formed a Popular Front. The polarization of political forces which ensued was reflected in the virtual annihilation of the Centre parties. The Radicals dropped from 105 to 5, whilst the swing to the Left played into the hands of the extra-parliamentary Falange on the other wing.

Up till then the Falange had not been a serious political force. It owed its existence in the first place to the filial piety of José Antonio Primo de Rivera who entered politics to defend the memory of his father from republican attacks. In 1932 he founded the Falange which two years later merged with another right-wing group, the Nazi-influenced JONS. Until 1936 it failed to make any progress except among university students and a small section of the working class in Seville, Cádiz and Madrid. The established parties of the Right shunned it, denouncing José Antonio as a Bolshevik, but the party was able to keep going with the funds of Bilbao industrialists who thought, as Hugenberg's Nationalists in Germany did of Hitler, that José Antonio could be bought. When it was clear he was not for sale, he was dropped. Only in the polarization of forces after the Popular Front victory, when it began to draw supporters away from the CEDA, did the Falange become respectable to the Right. Even then it remained on the fringe of the plots which were being hatched in the spring of 1936 by the Traditionalists, the monarchists and the right-wing military UME. General Mola, who, with Franco, believed in civilian assistance (against those who believed in a 'pure' military rising) considered the Carlists worth much closer cultivation than the Falangists.

When the rising finally came in July 1936 it was the work of a caucus of officers who assumed that a liberal-bourgeois government which had held the left-wing parties at arm's length would not arm the people. In this they were nearly correct, but finally, under pressure, arms were issued to the party militias. Nineteenth-century theories of a *pronunciamiento* by the military were no longer applicable in the social situation of the 1930s. Faulty planning alone cannot explain the failure of the army to make a swift takeover; it was due rather to the generals' mistaken assumption that political life was still, as formerly, the monopoly of politicians.

The Civil War and the Franco Régime

It was in October 1936 when the initial military coup had failed that General Franco, a member of the ruling Nationalist junta and commander of the Army of the South, assumed supreme direction of the Nationalist forces. He had first attracted attention by his military ability; a fiercely professional officer, uninterested in politics, he had risen through the Foreign Legion to become the army's youngest general. Already by 1934, as Minister of War, he had acquired a reputation on the Right as the saviour of the nation for his suppression of the Asturian rising, and his offer to the government of army support to prevent the Popular Front from taking power showed him in his true light – authoritarian and ready to assume the self-appointed role of defender of the 'essence of Spain'. If Primo's reputation for *hombría* was based on the less reputable aspects of virility, that of Franco was rooted in the legend of his bravery and his harsh humourless discipline. With his Gallegan caution he was far removed from the stereotype of the 'typical Spaniard', but cold-shouldering by the rest of Europe after 1939 enabled him to tap the deep sources of national xenophobia.

With the misfiring of the military revolt civil war was inevitable. The failure of certain garrisons to rise divided the country between the republicans controlling roughly the east, the north and most of the centre of Spain, and the Nationalists (as the rebels were called) controlling the western part of Andalusia and the far west of the country. Although the republicans dominated the larger area, including the industrial potential of Catalonia and the Basque provinces and enormous gold reserves, the Nationalists had superiority in arms and men. Two-thirds of the army, including the crack Army of Africa, two-thirds of the Civil Guard, the Carlist *requetés* from Navarre and Falangist levies, were matched against a minority of the army, the rest of the Civil Guard, the republican police (the *Asaltos*) and the untrained anarchist and socialist militias. Republican naval superiority was offset by the desertion or killing of officers. In the early days the air force was not an effective fighting force.

Popular enthusiasm on the republican side could not outweigh the military skill of the nationalist generals. Furthermore, war was the signal for the long-postponed anarchist social revolution which, in Catalonia at least, diverted attention from the war effort and caused divisions among the government's supporters. The communists, who had been unable to make any substantial headway against the anarchists or socialists since their foundation in 1921, came out in defence of the persecuted middle class without whose co-operation the war effort would have been doomed, and international communism also helped to redress the military balance by dispatching the International Brigades. The first of these arrived in Madrid on the day after the battle commenced and stiffened resistance. Madrid held out for three years and in view of the stalemate on the central front, the Nationalists concentrated on drives to the north and to clear the southern coast.

As had occurred in the 1830s, civil war soon involved the European powers. Within a week Franco recognized the need for foreign aid and put out feelers to Italy and Germany. From early August aid from these two countries started arriving in substantial quantities. Italian support was motivated by strategic ambitions to dominate the western Mediterranean by controlling the Balearics. A few cheap military victories might also be picked up at a time when the Abyssinian campaign was entering an unromantic phase. German interest was more complex. Strategy played its part although there were divisions over this between Nazi radicals and the conservative military. Economic interest, however, was a decisive factor as Spain could provide raw materials for the German rearmament programme as well as an opportunity to perfect untried methods of warfare. Hitler hoped that the war could be prolonged so as to perpetuate the distrust between France and Britain, on one side, and Italy, on the other, thus forcing Mussolini into a German alliance. Whereas Italy provided some 60,000 troops of doubtful military value, Germany contributed key technical advisers and specialized units of dive-bombers and anti-tank gunners.

On the republican side the cautious non-intervention policy of France and Britain led the government to turn to Russia which readily provided technical and political advisers and considerable war material in addition to the International Brigades. The resultant balance between the two sides led to a war of attrition and both the rebels and the government impressed mass support by means of terror. Finally, superior military skill and equipment, the gradual withdrawal of Russian assistance, and the deeper divisions on the republican side, enabled the Nationalists to triumph.

The régime which emerged at the end of the civil war was not one which sought a basis in reconciliation. The victors not only divided the spoils but despoiled the vanquished. Franco's greatest asset was the memory of the war; so long as this remained green Spaniards would accept repression, and his régime flourished on exhaustion and fear of further conflict. When the European war broke out in 1939, therefore, Franco's policy of neutrality heartened his supporters and depressed his opponents, who had hoped for Allied intervention. In marked contrast to Cánovas del Castillo after the Carlist war of the 1870s, no attempt was made to heal the wounds; regionalist aspirations were crushed, Protestants and freemasons were treated with the same severity as 'Reds'. The instrument of repression was the Falange which, in the immediate post-war period, saw its opportunity to fill the ideological vacuum with its own peculiar brand of mystical nationalism. It would nevertheless be mistaken to describe Franco's Spain as a 'one-party state' or a totalitarian dictatorship on the Italian model. Generals are not good ideologues and Franco, like Primo de Rivera, was no exception. The Falange, with its corporatism, served a useful purpose by providing a framework in place of the Liberal institutions which, for the Right, had been the cause of Spain's decay; but it never enjoyed complete control. Since José Antonio's death in a republican prison in 1936 no one had succeeded in dominating the party. The arch-pragmatist Franco had no time for the radical idealism of Hedilla, José Antonio's successor, and he drew the teeth of the Falange by forcing it to unite with the Carlists, so bequeathing a new crop of internal dissensions to an already deeply divided movement.

Falangism was useful as a check to the royalists, and it brought a certain amount of working class support; but it was only one factor in the equation of power which had to be worked out between the Government, the Army and the Church. The Army had always looked askance at the Falange and the Church disliked the strong anti-clerical streak which the radical wing has never foresworn. In spite of lip-service to Falangist doctrine, Franco's position therefore rested on a balance between these three forces. However, now that Franco is trying to edge Spain into a conservative big business Europe, Falangism is becoming a liability and for this reason official backing seems to be behind the Opus Dei's encroachment on Falangist preserves – particularly in the universities.

The structure of the régime as laid down in the Charter of Labour in 1938, the Law of 1942, the *Fuero de los Españoles* of 1945 and the Succession Law of 1947 was that of a Roman Catholic, organic and representative democracy, and the word 'Dictatorship' was reserved to describe Primo de Rivera's régime. The revived Cortes, elected by professional corporations, is a rubber stamp and labour, organized into vertical government-controlled syndicates, has been emasculated. Franco is committed to the restoration of the monarchy, but whether in the person of the exiled pretender Don Juan, favoured by constitutional monarchists, or of Don Juan's son, Don Carlos, army-trained and Falangist-influenced, remains uncertain. For the past twenty-five years Spain has experienced a period of political quietude.

With a change of ruler it may be that issues which were left unresolved thirty years ago will once again break surface and Spain's history may become as troubled as that of emerging countries which, although often sharing similar economic problems, suffer from an imperial legacy of a very different kind.

BIBLIOGRAPHY

The most stimulating introduction to modern Spanish history is Gerald Brenan's classic *Spanish Labyrinth* (2nd ed., Cambridge, 1950, also paperback). A fundamental work to appear in 1965 will be R. Carr, *A History of Modern Spain* (Oxford). S. de Madariaga's *Spain* (London, 1942) is challenging and liberal in tone. A readable leftist treatment is A. Ramos Oliveira, *Politics, Economics and Men of Modern Spain, 1808–1946* (Gollancz, 1946). For economic history J. Vicens Vives, *Historia social y económica de España y America*, vol. IV, part ii (Barcelona, 1959), is reliable and finely illustrated, whilst the best treatment of nineteenth-century Catalonia is his *Cataluña en el siglo XIX* (Madrid, 1961).

The nineteenth century has been grossly neglected by historians. Butler Clarke, *Modern Spain* (Cambridge, 1906), is old fashioned but thorough. C. A. M. Hennessy, *The Federal Republic in Spain, 1868–74* (Oxford, 1962), is a detailed analysis of the federal republican movement examined through the career of its inflexible leader Pi y Margall. The early Restoration can be studied in A. Houghton, *Les origines de la Restauration des Bourbons en Espagne* (Paris, 1890). For the crucial Cuban question there is in English only Guerra y Sanchez (et al.), *A History of the Cuban Nation* (Havana, 1958), vols. iv, v, vi.

Apart from R. Carr *Spain: Rule by Generals* in M. Howard, *Soldiers and Governments* (London, 1959), there is nothing on the crucial problem of the soldier in politics. There are no biographies of nineteenth or early twentieth century Spanish politicians in English. In Spanish, F. Almagro, *Cánovas* (Madrid, 1951), J. Pabon, *Cambó* (Madrid, 1952) and A. Sevilla, *Maura* (Madrid, 1954) can be recommended. The few hagiographical royal biographies in English will not bear close study. On the Restoration proper and the dictatorship there is no work in English although J. B. Trend, *The Origins of Modern Spain* (Cambridge, 1934), discusses some of the nineteenth-century thinkers who formed the modern Spanish liberal conscience. A. Barea, *Unamuno* (Cambridge, 1952), and J. Ferrater Mora, *Ortega y Gasset* (Cambridge, 1956), are useful for these two formative thinkers, whilst the latter's *Invertebrate Spain* (London, 1937) is an interesting interpretative essay. In Spanish, G. Maura, *Por que cayó Alfonso XIII* (Madrid, 1948), is a key study of the break-up of the party system; the same author's *La Dictadura* (Madrid, 1930) is the best survey of the dictatorship.

Neglect by English-speaking historians of modern Spain is best shown by the absence still of any detailed study of the all-important and fascinating Second Republic. G. Jackson, 'The Azaña régime in perspective', *American Historical Review* lxiv (1959), is a useful analysis.

F. Sedwick, *The tragedy of Manuel Azaña* (Ohio, 1963), is of limited interest. S. Payne, *Falange* (Oxford, 1962), is thorough and penetrating and is required reading for an understanding of 'Spanish Fascism'. A liberal Catholic treatment of 1934 is in A. Mendizabal, *The Martyrdom of Spain* (London, 1938). Two autobiographies are recommended, A. Barea, *The Forging of a Rebel* (New York, 1947), and A. del Vayo, *The last optimist* London, 1950).

There is a mass of material on the Civil War. Two classics are G. Orwell, *Homage to Catalonia* (London, 1938, and later editions), and F. Borkenau, *The Spanish Cockpit* (London, 1937, and paperback). H. Thomas, *The Spanish Civil War* (London, 1961), is a lively narrative, to which Broue and Témime, *La Révolution et la Guerre d'Espagne* (Paris, 1961), is a useful addition. The Left has been treated thoroughly in D. Catell, *Communism and the Spanish Civil War* (California, 1955), and in his *Soviet Diplomacy and the Spanish Civil War* (California, 1957), and by B. Bolloten, *The Grand Camouflage* (London, 1961). K. W. Watkins, *Britain Divided* (London, 1963), examines the reactions to the Civil War in Britain. S. Payne, *The Civil War in Spain* (London, 1962), is a useful collection of eye-witness accounts. A handy guide to the vast polemical literature is H. R. Southworth, *El Mito de la cruzada de Franco* (Paris, 1963).

Two books which are required reading on modern Spain are J. A. Pitt Rivers, *People of the Sierras* (London, 1954), and M. Kenny, *A Spanish Tapestry: Town and Country in Castille* (London, 1961). These works by social anthropologists throw great light on some of the premisses of Spanish behaviour. E. J. Hobsbawm, *Primitive Rebels* (Manchester, 1959), in addition to a chapter on the Casas Viejas affair, has also some stimulating thoughts on south European agrarian movements in general.

Franco Spain has been little studied in depth. A. P. Whitaker's *Spain and the Defence of the West* (Praeger, 1961, and paperback), is a useful survey, whilst P. Blanshard, *Freedom and Catholic Power in Spain and Portugal* (London, 1961), highlights some of the anomalies of the régime's religious policies. A useful study for the religious background is J. M. Sanchéz, *Reform and Reaction: the politico - religious background of the Spanish Civil War* (North Carolina, 1964).